Know About
Mother Teresa

KNOW ABOUT MOTHER TERESA

ALL RIGHTS RESERVED. No part of this book may be reproduced in a retrieval system or transmitted in any form or by any means electronics, mechanical, photocopying, recording and or without permission of the publisher.

Published by

MAPLE PRESS PRIVATE LIMITED
office: A-63, Sector 58, Noida 201301, U.P., India
phone: +91 120 455 3581, 455 3583
email: info@maplepress.co.in
website: www.maplepress.co.in

Reprinted in 2019

ISBN: 978-93-50334-09-6

Contents

Preface 5
1. Early Years 6
2. The First Call 10
3. The Teacher 14
4. The Second Call 18
5. The Missionaries of Charity 22
6. The Mother House 25
7. Health Issues and the Demise of Mother 28
8. Nirmal Hriday 31
9. Other Foundations 34
10. Other Charities 37
11. On Divorce 40
12. Thoughts on Abortion 43
13. The Power of Prayer 46
14. Prayers for the Soul 49
15. Prayers for Christ and Mother Mary 54
16. Submitting to the Almighty 57
17. More about the Missionaries of Charity 60
18. Honours Conferred on Mother 64
19. Nobel Prize Speech 67
20. Famous Quotes 70
21. Doctrines of the Mother 73
21. Chronology 76

Preface

One of the most respected women of the 20th century, Mother Teresa was the epitome of love, care and affection. She got inclined towards divinity at a tender age and was unable to see the pain of others. Thus, she made the firm decision to dedicate her life in the service of God and his beings. She found a religious order of nuns in Calcutta, India which was known as the Missionaries of Charity. Through this order, she helped the sick, poor and dying people of the country as well as the entire world with unwavering faith and devotion. She selflessly worked for the needy people and was rewarded for her unending enthusiasm. She won the Nobel Peace Prize in 1979 and recently the Pope of Rome canonized her. Mother has shown by her example that humanity still resides on earth and God can come to the aid of his children in any form.

CHAPTER 1
Early Years

On August 26, 1910, when a frail child was born in an Albanian family, little did they know that the girl child was to build an empire of love in her later years. She was to prove to the world that with love everything can be conquered in this world. She was like a mother to the poor, who showered her love on the unloved and cared for the ones who were left alone by their kin. She was none other than Anjezë Gonxhe Bojaxhiu better known as Mother Teresa. According to the Catholic customs of those days, she was baptized on 27 August, 1910 at Skopje, in Macedonia.

Little Anjezë imbibed the first lesson in charity at her home, from her parents Kole and Drana and held true the age old proverb – 'Charity begins at home.' Her father was a grocer and also owned a building company. He was interested in politics and was a member of the community council. He travelled a lot and was a multilingual person. In 1919, when Anjezë was only nine years old, her father died. Hence, Drana was left to raise her three children,

Aga (1904), Lazar (1907) and Anjezë (1910), all alone. This was undoubtedly quite a difficult task for a woman in those days. She took to sewing and embroidering wedding dresses, and somehow managed to educate her children. Drana was a devout Christian. Every evening, she and her children would go to church, pray with the rosary and assist in the service of the Holy Virgin. They also followed the tenets of the Lord with full dedication. Every poor and needy person, who knocked at their door, was given proper attention and care. Drana also took care of her

neighbours. She went to feed and wash an alcoholic, twice a day. She also took care of a widow and her six children. After the death of the widow, her children were raised by Drana, as a part of her family. During the holidays, Drana and her children used to follow a custom of the family. They would stay in a holy place in Letina.

Anjezë was very fond of reading, singing and praying. She liked to spend most of her time in the company of God

in the church. She also enjoyed doing all the charitable work in the absence of her mother. Anjezë studied well and went to Lyceum, Lazar won a scholarship in Austria and Aga followed commercial school. Together with Aga, she was in the Choir. She was a soprano and Aga, the second voice. She also played the mandolin.

When Anjezë was a twelve-year-old girl, she used to help the Father, who had difficulties with the language, to teach Catechism. She read a lot about Slovenian and Croatian missionaries in India. And this is what inspired in her a strong desire to spend her life in the service of mankind.

CHAPTER 2

The First Call

As soon as the desire of serving the poor and the needy became strong in Anjezë, she began to contemplate about it seriously. She discussed about it with her mother and her sisters. She prayed to God to guide her to the path of service to Him in particular, and to humanity, in general. It was the first call from God to her.

In the meantime, she often went to church to ask the Father how she can be sure of following the path that leads to God. Father answered, "Through your joy. If you think that you will be blessed if you get a call from God to serve Him and your neighbours, then it is proof enough that God is calling you indeed." And then he added, "The depth of your inner joy, the feeling of peace and tranquility is the compass that indicates the direction of your life."

Finally, at the age of eighteen, she took the decision to follow the path of service to God and her fellow beings. She assisted several religious retreats in Letnice and after that she decided to become a missionary and go to India. The

Sisters of Our Lady of Loreto was a religious congregation that was very active in India at that time. She decided to join this congregation. In 1928, on Assumption day, she went to Letnice to pray for Our Lady's blessing before leaving.

On September 25, she left her native place. The whole neighbourhood including her friends, schoolmates, and of course, her mother and her sister Aga went to the station to see her off. Needless to say it was a tearful farewell.

She travelled over Zagreb, to Austria, Switzerland, France, to London and reached the motherhouse of Loreto sisters, which is located in Abbey, near Dublin. Here Anjezë got trained in religious life and English. She received the clothes of a sister and chose the name of Sister Teresa, in the memory of the Little Teresa of Lisieux.

On December 1, 1928, she left for India, after her papers got ready. There were also some more sisters on board with her in the long and tiring journey. For weeks, they religiously prayed with the rosary and sang Christmas songs. They could not attend mass or receive communion, not even on Christmas.

In the beginning of 1929, they reached Colombo, then Madras and finally, Calcutta. The journey continued to Darjeeling, at the feet of the Himalayas, where the young sister accomplished her training. On May 23, 1929, she was accepted as a novice and two years later, she made her first vows. Immediately after that, she was sent to Bengal, to help the sisters in the little hospital that catered to the needs of the sick, starving and helpless mothers. She was touched by the endless misery which she saw there.

CHAPTER 3
The Teacher

At the beginning of her career in India, Mother Teresa was trained in Calcutta to become a teacher. But as always, whenever she got time, she used to take care of the sick.

On her way to school as a teacher, she had to cross the city everyday and hence, she constantly bore witness to the misery that was there in the streets of Calcutta. After reaching school, her first work was to clean the classroom,

which very few teachers did in those days. Quickly, the children started loving her for her enthusiasm and tenderness and their number rose to three hundred.

Soon, she was made the headmistress of a secondary school for the middle class Bengali girls. She taught history and geography for some time. But Mother was not happy with this because, near her institute was one of the greatest slums of Calcutta. Sister Teresa would often close her eyes and think, "Who cares for these poor people living in the streets?" The letters from her mother advised her about the great charity and she recalled that she had received the basic call to care for the sick and the poor. She saw where they lived and what they ate. She started taking care of them whenever she had time. Soon, they began to call her 'ma' due to her care and love.

The Legion of Mary was also active in the school where Mother Teresa taught. With the girls, Sister Teresa regularly visited hospitals, slums and the poor people. She realized that the people, whom she visited, did not pray at all. They talked quite seriously about what they saw and what they did. The Belgian Walloon Jesuit, Father Henry, who was a spiritual director, proved to be a great inspiration in this work and directed Sister Teresa for several years. Under his inspiration, Sister Teresa acquired the desire to do more for the poor. But she did not know how.

With all these things going on in her head, she left for a retreat to Darjeeling on the 10th of September. She

afterwards referred to this journey as, "the most important journey of my life." It was then that she really heard God's voice. His message was clear that she had to leave the convent, in order to help the poorest of the poor and live with them. Later, Mother said, "It was an order, a duty, an absolute certainty that I knew what to do, but I did not know how." Till date, the 10th of September is considered so important in the Society that it is called the 'Inspiration day'.

Finally, it was on May 24, 1937, that Sister Teresa took her final vows.

CHAPTER 4
The Second Call

Sister Teresa heard the call from God to serve humanity. She prayed hard for His guidance. She then talked with some other sisters and asked her superior about it. She in turn sent Sister Teresa to see the archbishop of Calcutta, Mgr. Perrier. But, unfortunately, he refused to permit her initially. But then he considered it seriously and talked it over with Father Henry and Father Celeste Van Exem S.J., who knew Sister Teresa well. They considered thoroughly the problems associated with the situation. One of the principal dilemmas was that India was about to become independent and Sister Teresa was a European. Besides this, there were political and other dangers as well. They were even concerned about Rome's reaction over the decision. The bishop told Sister Teresa to think over this decision for at least a year, or join the Daughters of Saint Anna, sisters wearing a dark blue sari and working among the poor. Sister Teresa did not consider this to be the right response for her. She wanted to live among the poor and serve them. When after a year, Sister Teresa renewed her intentions, the archbishop wanted to grant her the permission, but decided it would be better to get the permission from Rome and from the Mother General in Dublin. This decision took a long time.

In August 1948, after a long delay, Sister Teresa received the permission to leave the Loreto community, under the condition to keep "the vows of poverty, purity and obedience." She was 38, when she bid adieu to her sisters and religious Loreto robe, to change into a cheap

white and blue sari to identify herself with the poorest of the poor.

Immediately afterwards she went to Patna and followed a nursing training with the sisters there. It was obvious to her that she could only help the poor in their dirty, sickening habitations, by knowing how to prevent and cure diseases. Thus, she realized that it was absolutely essential to undergo a medical training in order to fulfill her call. Her superior in Patna, a doctor, gave her a good advice when she talked to him about her desire to live among the poor and care for them. When Sister Teresa said that she wanted to live on rice and salt, like the poor, the superior answered that such a diet would hinder her in following her call, and the kind of life that she had chosen demanded a strong and good health.

Back in Calcutta, Sister Teresa visited the slums and streets to talk to the poor and help them. All she had with her was a piece of soap and five rupees. She helped in washing the babies and cleaning the wounds. Soon, she started teaching the poor children how to read and write and how to wash and be hygienic. Later, she was able to hire a small place to make a school.

She herself slept with the Sisters of the Poor. Her only refuge was the Almighty towards whom she looked up for strength and material support. And He truly was with her, as she always found the right medicine, clothes, food and a place to receive the poor, so that she could help them.

CHAPTER 5
The Missionaries of Charity

One day a Bengali girl, from a well-off family and former student of Sister Teresa, approached her and revealed her desire to stay with her and help her. This was a touching moment, but Sister Teresa was realistic and she spoke to the girl about the poverty and the disagreeable aspects of the work. She proposed that the girl must think over her decision again and wait for some time.

On March 19, 1949, the girl returned to Sister Teresa with no jewels and in a poor dress. The decision was made. She was the first to join Sister.

Soon many other girls followed. In May, they were three, in November five and the next year, their number rose to seven. And Sister Teresa prayed for more girls to join in the service of the Lord and Our Lady. There was a lot of work to do. The sisters woke up early in the morning and spent their time in prayers for a long time and worshipped the Lord. Then they attended the mass so that they could find in their spiritual life the strength to do the material work in the service of the poor. As the

community started growing, Mr. Michael Gomes offered the top floor of his house to Sister Teresa so that the sisters could live and work. In the same year, Sister Teresa took the Indian nationality.

Sister Teresa noticed that the community was growing at a considerable rate and thought that she could now think about starting a congregation. For the first constitutions, she asked the advice of two of her first helpers, Father Julien Henry S.J. and Father Celest Van Exem S.J. The last reading was done by Father P. De Gheldere. Thus, 'Constitutions of the Society of the Missionaries of Charity' was presented to the archbishop, who sent it to Rome for approval.

Early in autumn, the papal's approval arrived and on October 7, 1950, the feasting of the Holy Rosary was done and the foundation ceremony was celebrated in the chapel of the sisters.

The archbishop displayed his support by celebrating mass and then the foundation papers were read by Father Van Exem. The community comprised of 12 sisters at that time. Thereafter, every year, hundreds of sisters all over the world celebrate on the feast day of Our Lady of the Rosary, the foundation of the Congregation. Not even five years after this day, the congregation became papal, which meant that they were directly under the control of the Pope.

It is the basic rule in the Rule of the Society that the sisters, out of love for Jesus, devote themselves, out of their free will, to the service of the poor and the needy. In fact, it is considered to be their fourth vow. In this way, they work for the salvation and sanctification of the poor.

CHAPTER 6
The Mother House

Mother's charitable work grew in leaps and bounds. More and more poor and sick people came to ask for help and the free devotion of the sisters was admired by everyone. Finding a suitable house to accept the increasing number of sisters was becoming a necessity. After a novena to Saint Cecilia, the solution came across. A Muslim, who was leaving the town for Pakistan, sold his big house for

a cheap price and it became the famous 'Mother house' at Lower Circular Road 54A.

The nuns first came from Bengal and then from all over India and finally, from all over the world. The founder herself was a novice mistress. One of the Fathers were asked to provide a spiritual training. But when it came to any other matter concerning the house and the Community, Mother made it very clear that she did not want any interference from outside.

The Society was growing rapidly and Mother continuously prayed for vocations and the work was appreciated by one and all. Some houses were opening and some were closing down, from one day to another, due to some or other political, social or security reason. The Society was very much alive and moving. Mother Teresa went all over the world to help people, rescue children

and advised her sisters, to organize a meeting and talk to the poor. She was again and again asked to address words to a group of sometimes 'ordinary' and sometimes very 'exquisite' crowds. In spite of the fact that her message was often the same and could be captured in a few sentences and she certainly had many a times, a quite 'traditional' point of view, she was listened to carefully. In spite of her age, she continued to search for resources to help the poor people all over the world and she always helped them with whatever she had at her disposal. Her sisters are present in every continent, including Russia, serving the needy for the love of Jesus.

Mother Teresa was well-versed in five languages – Albanian, English, Hindi, Bengali and Serbian. Due to this reason she often went to other countries in order to reach the people who were left miserable through the trick of fate. By 1996, she was operating 517 missions in over 100 countries.

CHAPTER 7
Health Issues and the Demise of Mother

Mother Teresa was a spiritual leader who has left a mark on the world. But like all human beings, she too faced the problems of old age. While visiting Pope John Paul II in Rome in 1983, Mother suffered a heart attack. A second attack followed in 1989 and she was provided with an artificial pacemaker.

In 1991, she was in Mexico when she was down with pneumonia that further increased her heart problems. In 1992, by the election of the New Superior general, she was prepared to hand over the responsibility as the head of the Missionaries of Charity. But, she was re-elected and continued with her services.

In April 1996, she broke her collarbone and four months later suffered from malaria. Her heart was weakening and she underwent a heart surgery but this time her health had started to fail seriously. She now expressed that she would not be able to continue her services as the head. Hence on March 13, 1997, the assembly of sisters elected Sister Nirmala to continue the beautiful work of the Mother.

Sadly the day dawned when the best loved women of the century left the world with thousands of her followers and admirers mourning in despair. Mother died on September

5, 1997, at the age of 87. The funeral services of Mother Teresa took place on September 13, 1997. Coincidentally, it was also the 51st anniversary of her receiving the divine order. About hundred nuns of the Missionaries of Charity, wearing their traditional blue-trimmed saris, gathered around the flower-covered grave, in a former dining hall of the convent, where Mother Teresa lived. Needless to say that all of them felt a vacuum after her death, but her work continues... thanks to the sisters who are her ardent followers.

At the time of her death, there were over 4,000 sisters in the Missionaries of Charity and the congregation was associated with 300 members with an operation of 610 missions in 123 countries.

Mother Teresa was beatified on 19 October 2003 by Pope John Paul II at Saint Peter's Square, Vatican City and has been canonized recently at the same place on 4 September 2016 by Pope Francis.

CHAPTER 8
Nirmal Hriday

One of the first foundations of Mother Teresa in Calcutta was the 'Home for the Dying Destitute', which she called the Nirmal Hriday (the Home of the Pure Heart). In an interview with Malcolm Muggeridge, Sister Teresa had told how for the first time she picked up a woman from the street:

"I found more people dying in the street. The employee of health services brought me to the temple of Kali and

showed me the 'dormashalah', where the pilgrims used to rest after they worshipped the Goddess Kali. The building was empty and he asked me if I wanted it. I was very glad with the offer for many reasons, but especially because it was the centre of prayer for Hindus. Within 24 hours, we brought our sick and suffering and started the Home for the Dying Destitute."

Ever since thousands of men, women and children (more than 40, 000) were taken from the streets in Calcutta and transported to the home. Half of them died in a kind surrounding. They were provided with both human and divine love in their last hours so that they could feel that they were also dear to God who loved them as His own children. For those who did not die, the sisters tried to find a job or they were sent to homes where they could live happily for some more years in a homely surrounding.

'Home for the Dying Destitute' became more and more famous. It was a daily affair with the sisters to pick up the dying from the street and to bring them to this house, when there was nowhere else for them to go. They were washed, freshly dressed and put into bed with the proper medical care and with tender and patient attention.

All over India and the world, the 'Missionaries of Charity' have homes for the dying and the very sick people, who have nobody else to care or who cannot pay for any medical help. The sisters have ambulances, doctors, nurses, etc. Apart from this, many friends and volunteers give a helping hand to the charity work of the great lady.

The following is a version of the kind of work they do in the words of the Mother herself, "We are not social workers or social assistants. We want to bring the joy and love of God to the people; we want to bring them God Himself, who gives them His love through us. At the same time, we love God and show Him our love, by serving Him in his people. There are a lot of institutions caring for the sick. We do not want to be one among them. We are not one or another organisation of social service, we have to be more, to give more, we have to give ourselves. We have to bring God's love to the people by our service. And, the poor people have taught us, what it really means to love and to serve God, although our full understanding will only come after we die."

CHAPTER 9
Other Foundations

Shishu Bhavan

Another early foundation of the Missionaries of Charity was 'Shishu Bhavan', a home for the babies. Many of the children residing here either do not have parents or have parents, who cannot care for them and thus, do not want them. According to a sister from the organisation, "Some, we pick up from the street, others are brought to

us from hospitals, where they were left behind by their parents. Some come from the prisons and others are brought by policemen. No matter how they come here, we have never refused a child till now."

At present, in India alone, there are over forty houses for children. Not only here, but all over the world too, the sisters have children's homes where they are taken care of by the sisters. A common belief is that the children brought and raised at Shishu Bhavan are handicapped children. But it is untrue. Some have studied and got married, have important social roles, and themselves became the messengers of love, doing good to people around them.

Shanti Nagar

Lepers are an important episode in the life story of Mother Teresa. India, as you all know, has quite a great number of lepers. The position of a leper is far from enviable in India. In the traditional mentality, this disease is a punishment by God and thus, one has to accept and suffer the disease without complaint. Lepers are banned from the society, even if they are very rich or highly educated. They lose their work and their family, escape to the mountains as a necessity and beg for their food. They live and die like animals.

When Mother Teresa explained that this was a disease that, in many cases, could be cured and not a punishment, all she got was cold responses. Undaunted by all these, Mother started to make small villages, where the lepers could live and work in peace and be cared for, but she needed to find a proper place.

She appealed to the millions of inhabitants of the city of Calcutta with the plea, "Touch the leper with your kindness". Through this she collected a huge amount of money. With this money, added to other donations, she created Shanti Nagar, 'The city of peace', where sick and healed lepers are cared for, helped to learn a skill and find work.

Mother Teresa was especially kind to these lepers, who were unloved, uncared and unwanted in the society. Once she said, "When I touch the smelling body I know I touch the body of Christ, as I receive Him in the Holy Communion under the sign of bread."

CHAPTER 10
Other Charities

During her lifetime, Mother's work had spread very fast. The sisters are now active all over India, and in many countries of the world, from Venezuela to Jordan, from Italy to Tanzania, from the United States to Russia. More and more bishops asked for sisters and the number of vocations increased, especially in India. Mother Teresa considered the prospect of expansion and discussed it with the members of the clergy before giving her consent.

She opened a house for alcoholics, drug addicts, the homeless and the destitute in Rome. The Pope also asked her to open a house for mothers with unwanted pregnancies. A second noviciate was set up in Rome in order to deal with the vocations from Europe and America. In the spirit of the second Vatican council, she accepted non-Christian novices in India, under the condition that they would accept the life and engagement of the 'Missionaries of Charity' with full commitment. As said, with the changes in the communist countries, she opened houses in such countries as Russia, Poland, Croatia, etc.

Soup Kitchen

In many big cities, where the homeless and the lost have no place to go or stay and certainly nobody to care, the sisters have a soup kitchen every day. Thus, such men and women can have a warm meal and a warm place and good food there.

Most of the time, they end up becoming a small family and care for each other with all their hearts. The sisters also cook for them on feast days like Christmas, Easter, etc., with the help of volunteers.

Rehabilitation of the prisoners

Mother Teresa has given ample support to the project of rehabilitation of the prisoners. At the opening of the second convention of the 'ministers in prisons', she said, "It is a beautiful gift of god to take care of men and women in prison." There were around 50 religious priests who

attended the function and out of them, more than 20 were volunteers and worked on the rehabilitation of the prisoners. During the function, Mother Teresa recalled her first encounter with this world, when the government of West Bengal asked her help for the imprisoned female prostitutes. It is to be mentioned that the Catholic Community in Calcutta took the initiative for this.

In the early 80s, the world was rocked by the detection of the disease called AIDS that killed hundreds of young people, and on which very few information was available. Many of those suffering from this deadly disease were left aside in the hospitals or had become unwanted. It was again Mother Teresa, who brought and showed the great love of the one she had devoted her life to, Jesus. She opened homes for the AIDS patients all over the world.

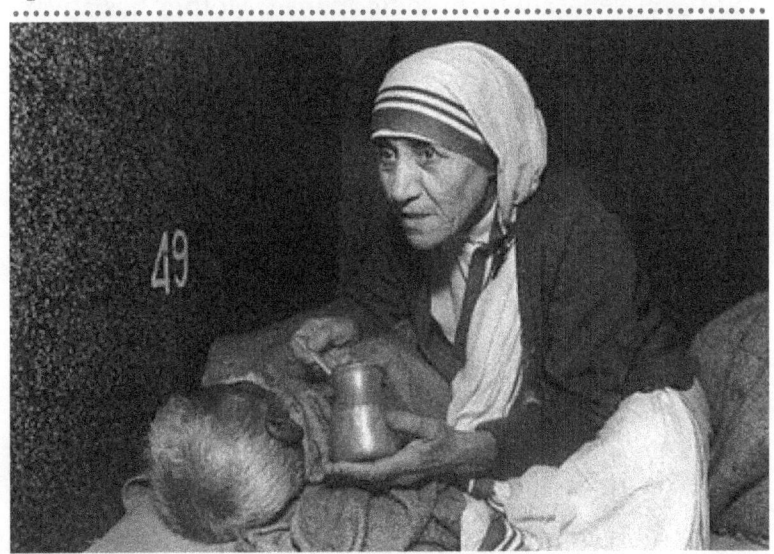

CHAPTER 11
On Divorce

Mother Teresa was strictly against the concept of divorce. She believed in the principle advocated by the Bible that states that when a man gets united with his wife then the two persons become one soul. This unification of a man and a woman in the bond of love and marriage is the order of God and people must not go against His wishes and never separate from their spouse. Mother has always advised couples who face any kind of trouble in their married life to pray to God individually and together as a family. Divorce has never been supported by Catholic teachings and therefore, Mother Teresa encouraged people to love with pure hearts. According to her, true love has no end and it is meant to unite two souls and not divide them. Love has the power to heal, to forgive and it lasts forever. Breaking a vow of marriage is equivalent to going against this universal power and the Almighty who made the union of two human beings.

If a marriage fails and the couple decides to separate, the major loss is suffered by the children. A husband and

wife may separate but a mother and father cannot. In both cases, people underestimate the power of love and go against the will of God and succumb to the powers of hatred. But love brings with it peace, joy and unity that maintains the cohesiveness of a family.

Mother considers divorce as the destroyer of love and further explains that it leads to loneliness and despair. If a person separates from their spouse they will go to their friends for relief but they may find that all the people of their age are married and happy with their spouses. There might be a possibility of the divorced person creating some misunderstanding between the couple and thus, hamper with their married life. Else, the person may find themselves uncomfortable in the presence of a couple.

According to Mother, even if there are problems and husband and wife do not love each other, they must live separately for some time but never take the decision of divorce as the final outcome.

Mother Teresa condemns the countries that allow divorce and states that broken families will break the society and shatter away the peace and happiness of the nation. Her suggestions may prove to be impractical in the current world scenario, but it is true that one must give a try to maintain the cordial relations and give their best to retain the love that is essential to a successful marriage.

CHAPTER 12
Thoughts on Abortion

Mother is also known for her strong opposition of the issue of abortion. When she received the Nobel Price for Peace in 1979, she described it as "the worst evil in the world." With all the moral authority she had earned through her life, she defended the right to a valuable life for every human being and especially, for the unborn.

According to her, life is a gift from God and nobody has the right to strip off this privilege from anyone, not

even the pregnant mother who wishes to abort her unborn child.

Mother Teresa felt that abortion was "the greatest destroyer of peace" in the whole world. It is unacceptable to think of a mother killing her own child and prioritizing her time and freedom at the cost of her child's life. Abortion is a war against the unborn child in the womb of a mother. Apart from her, it is the duty of the father as well not to participate in this crime of murdering his own child.

By aborting a child, the mother prefers to solve her own problems by killing the innocent child who has done no harm to anyone in the world. The father is given the liberty that he does not need to take any responsibility of the child who owes his existence to him equally. This might make him free and he may put other women in the

same trouble as well. Thus, it will become a never-ending process.

Mother Teresa further states that "countries that allow abortion are poor because they do not have the courage to accept one more life." Any country that accepts abortion does not teach its citizens love but rather appeals to them to use violence to get what they want. Abortion is a form of violence against one's own child and therefore, it is a sin committed against God.

Mother Teresa had even made adoption a measure against abortion. She said, "…anybody who doesn't want the child, please give it to me. I want the child." She offers to adopt the child and take good care of them, so that the child gets adopted by the couples who cannot have a child of their own. But she never allowed a child to get adopted by couples who had tried to destroy the child in the first place. According to her, "By adopting a child, these couples receive Jesus but, by aborting a child, a couple refuses to receive Jesus."

CHAPTER 13

The Power of Prayer

People often wondered where did Mother Teresa, the small creature in a cheap white sari, find the courage, the power and the strength to do what she did for so many years. And that seems to the world both genius and heroic. She was often asked this question, to which she replied, "The activity of the sisters, all what we do is only the fruit of prayer, of our unity with Jesus in the Eucharist. Thanks to this unity it is possible for us to spend ourselves in the service of the lepers, the dying, the children, the unwanted and many other people. When we come home in the evening, we have an hour of adoration. This is the biggest treasure of the Missionaries of Charity." From the beginning, the Society was a praying community. Mother advocated pray at home, pray on the street, pray during the work. Be active and contemplative at the same time.

With a great veneration to Our Lady, the yearly feast of the 7th of October is an Our Ladies feast, for the Sisters of religious life. Our Lady is for Mother Teresa the deeply venerated Heavenly Mother, who took the decision in

Letnice to devote herself, totally and without any reserve, to God.

She said, "If you pray with words, let them be filled with love and come from the deepest of your heart. Pray with great respect and trust. Fold your hands, close your eyes and lift up your heart to the Lord. Let your prayer be a pure sacrifice to God. Do not pray loud and not too quiet. Pray simply- Let your heart speak. Praise the Lord with all your soul."

"Words will come like that from the bottom of your heart and you will find joy in prayer. Stop once in a while by a word and think it over, let it sink to the bottom of your heart."

"Keep them during the rest of the day: they will bring you peace."

CHAPTER 14
Prayers for the Soul

The following are a few prayers sung by the Missionaries of Charity sisters.

The fruit

    The fruit of silence is prayer,

    The fruit of prayer is faith,

    The fruit of faith is love,

    The fruit of love is service,

    The fruit of service is peace.

Prayer from Pope Paul

Make us worthy, Lord, to serve our fellow men throughout the world, who live and die in poverty and hunger. Give them today, through our hands, their daily bread and through our understanding love, give peace and joy.

Feel often during the day the need for prayer and pray. Prayer opens the heart, till it is capable of containing God himself. Ask and seek and your heart will be big enough to receive Him and keep Him as Your Own.

Prayer from St. Francis

Lord, make me a channel of Your peace, that where there is hatred, I may bring love, where there is wrong, I may bring the spirit of forgiveness, where there is discord, I may bring harmony, where there is error, I may bring truth, where there is doubt, I may bring faith, where there is despair, I may bring hope, where there are shadows, I may bring light and where there is sadness, I may bring joy.

Lord, grant that I may comfort, rather than to be comforted, that I may understand, rather than to be understood that I may love, rather than to be loved.

For it is by forgetting self that one finds it is by forgiving that one is forgiven it is by dying that one awakens to eternal life.

Prayer for peace

Lead me from death to life,
from lies to truth
Lead me from despair to hope
from fear to trust
Lead me from hatred to love
from war to peace .
Let peace fill our heart, our world
our universe... peace, peace, peace.

The following is the prayer for the Holy Spirit, sung by the Missionaries of Charity sisters.

Breathe in me, O Holy Spirit that my thoughts may all be holy

Act in me, O Holy Spirit that my work too may be holy

Draw my heart, O Holy Spirit that I love but what is holy

Strengthen me, O Holy Spirit, to defend all that is holy

Guide me then, O Holy Spirit that I always may be holy.

Whatsoever you do
When I was hungry, you gave me to eat;
when I was thirsty you gave me to drink

Whatsoever you do to the least of my brethren, you do it to Me.

Come and enter the house of My Father.

When I was a stranger, you opened your doors;

when I was naked, you gave me clothes
When I was tired, you gave me peace;
when I was frightened, you calmed me down
When I was small, you taught me to read;
when I was lonely, you gave me your love
I was in prison, you visited me;

I was sick and you took care of me

In a strange country, you gave me a home;

when I had no job, you found me one

When I was wounded, you took care of it;

looking for friendship, you gave me your hand

Whether I was black or white or yellow; mocked at or insulted, you carried my cross

When I was old, you smiled at me; when I couldn't find peace, you brought it to me.

You saw me: full of spit and blood; dirty with sweat, still you said you knew me.

You were on my side in times of despise; in the hour of joy, we were together.

CHAPTER 15
Prayers for Christ and Mother Mary

Radiating Christ

Dear Jesus, help me to spread your fragrance everywhere I go. Flood my soul with Your spirit and life. Penetrate and possess my whole being so utterly that all my life may only be a radiance of yours.

Shine through me and be so in me that every soul I come in contact with may feel Your presence in my soul.

Let them look up and see no longer me but only Jesus! Stay with me and then I shall begin to shine as You shine, so to shine as to be a light to others; the light, O Jesus, will be all from You; none of it will be mine: it will be You shining on others through me.

Let me thus praise You in the way You love best: by shining on those around me. Let me preach You without preaching, not by words, but by my example, by the catching force, the sympathetic influence of what I do, the evident fullness of the love my heart bears to You.

Amen.

Prayer to our lady

Mary, Mother of Jesus, give me your heart so beautiful, so pure, so immaculate, so full of love and humility that I may be able to receive Jesus in the Bread of Life, love Him as You loved Him and serve Him as You served Him in the distressing disguise of the poorest of the poor. Amen.

Remember, o most gracious Virgin Mary that never was it known that anyone who fled to your protection, implored your help or sought your intercession was left unaided. Inspired with this confidence we fly to You, o virgin of the virgins, our Mother. To you we come, before you we stand sinful and sorrowful. O Mother of the word incarnate, despise not our petitions, but in your clemency, hear and answer us.

Amen.

Prayer for the society

Beseech Thee, O Lord mercifully poor into our Society
Thy Holy Spirit by whose wisdom it was created,
by whose providence it is governed and maintained
and whose love may kindle in the Society that same fire
which Our Lord Jesus Christ, sent down upon earth
earnestly desiring that it should burn mightily. And so
Breath in me, o Holy Spirit that my thoughts may be holy;
act in me, o Holy Spirit that my work may be holy;
draw my heart, o Holy Spirit that I love but what is holy;

strengthen me, o Holy Spirit, to defend all that is holy; guard me then, o Holy Spirit that always maybe holy. Amen.

CHAPTER 16
Submitting to the Almighty

The moral fibre of Mother as deciphered from the works and speeches of the great lady is as follows:

- Totally surrender to God's will. Find out what He wants, not what we would like to be or to do.
- Pray. Prayer is the way to listen to God, to speak with Him, to understand His love for us.
- Adoration and Eucharist. To love God and to learn to love Him more, it is necessary to be in His presence every day. This is done in the Eucharist: to receive His presence in us, in commemoration of His will. And through Adoration: to stay and be in His presence, contemplating His words and His life, so as to see His will over our lives.
- Take God on His words. The trust Mother has in God's promises, cannot be understood by people who do not believe in Him. And even for those who believe it is difficult to understand. She trusted Him like a child trusts his father.

- Serve and love one person at a time. God does not want us to love masses - that is impossible. He wants us to love Him in every single person we meet. (This is also very evident when you meet Mother. It is as if nobody else but you and she exist, though you are in the middle of a crowd. It is here that you feel God's presence in her.)

- Have a deep respect for every human creature because it is an image and the temple of God. (Hence, Mother fights against abortion for care and love of every human being.)
- Love begins at home: start to love and serve your family, your neighbours.
- Share with the poor and needy around you: a smile, a word, your time, your friendship, your belongings.
- Give God, the big 'Other', a capital place in your life: pray, meditate, adore.
- See God's presence in the people you meet daily and treat them as children of God.
- Do not waste a second of your time on useless and ugly things.
- Live according to God's standards on life (10 commandments).
- God's love is always present in your life. He loved you first and will love you always.

CHAPTER 17
More about the Missionaries of Charity

Branches of the Society

The Society has 8 branches and each one of them has houses in different countries. They are as follows:
- The active sisters (1950)
- The contemplative sisters, also called 'Sisters of the Word' (1976)
- The active brothers (1963 Muggeridge -1966 Vardey)
- The contemplative brothers
- The father's missionaries
- The Corpus Christi Movement for Priests
- The lay-missionaries (1986)
- The volunteers (1950 ever since the beginning they have come)
- The sick and suffering co-workers (1969)

The International Association of the Co-workers of Mother Teresa was started in 1969 and ended in 1994. In April 1997, Mother wrote a letter to all the co-workers to ask their opinion according to the organisation.

Training

Before deciding to join, a young woman or man can stay for some time in a convent and share the active life. This is called the 'come and see' period. After some serious talks with one of the sisters on your intentions, wishes and health, if the result is that you consider this life to be your way of life, you may join for the training. Sisters of the active and the contemplative branch have a training of six years, which can be divided into the following periods:

- Aspirancy - six months
- Postulancy - at most a year

- Noviciate - two years, at the end of which first vows are made and the girl/woman becomes a sister.
- Juniorate - five years, during which the vows are renewed each year. The vows are only renewed on request of the junior.
- Tertianship - one year, the sixth year after the first vows. Before her final vows at the end of this year, the sister returns home for three weeks to clearly think if she really wants to spend the rest of her life as a Missionary of Charity.
- Finally becomes a sister

Religious life

A day of the sisters is mostly like this:

4.30 a.m. getting up

5.00 a.m. morning prayer

6.00 a.m. spiritual reading and meditation

7.00 a.m. attending mass

7.30 a.m. breakfast

8.00 a.m. housework

9.00 a.m. apostolate

12.00 p.m. noon prayer

12.30 p.m. meal

1.00 p.m. Our Ladies Office

1.30 p.m. rest

2.00 p.m. tea

2.15 p.m. apostolate
5.15 p.m. adoration
7.00 p.m. time to wash clothes
7.30 p.m. meal
8.00 p.m. recreation
9.00 p.m. evening prayer
9.15 p.m. night prayer
9.30 p.m. bedtime

CHAPTER 18
Honours Conferred on Mother

Mother Teresa, the Macedonian born Catholic nun who spent her entire life caring for the poor in the slums of Calcutta, was voted as India's greatest citizen in a magazine poll.

In a survey published by a magazine, Mother Teresa was voted the greatest Indian since the country's independence in 1947, from a poll of more than 50,000 responses.

Mother Teresa had won the Nobel Peace Prize in 1979, was beatified in 2003 and canonized in 2016. In the poll records, she had beaten the charismatic leader of India, Jawaharlal Nehru, the first Prime Minister of the country, who had earned the second rank. Indira Gandhi, India's prime minister for 15 years, was placed fourth in the list of 10.

Prime Minister Atal Bihari Vajpayee gained the tenth position. The master blaster of the Indian cricket team was placed at the eighth position. The magazine did not include India's best-known citizen, Mohandas K. Gandhi, as they wished to 'keep the father of our nation above a voting process.'

"We are very happy and we are proud to hear this news," said Sister Nirmala, who heads Mother Teresa's order, the Missionaries of Charity, in Calcutta.

Other Awards

- 1971 Peace Price John xxiii
- 1971 Price of the Good Samaritan, Boston
- 1971 Kennedy Price
- 1972 Koruna Dut, angel of charity, President of India
- 1973 Templeton Price
- 1974 Mater et Magistra
- 1975 Albert Schweitzer International Price
- 1977 Doctor Honoris Causa in Theology, University of Cambridge
- 1979 Nobel Prize for Peace
- 1980 – Bharat Ratna, India's highest award for civilians
- 1982 Doctor Honoris Causa, Catholic University Brussels
- 1996 Honorary citizen of America (4th person to get this nomination)

CHAPTER 19
Nobel Prize Speech

Mother Teresa won the Nobel Peace Prize on 17 October 1979, for her compassionate work in the welfare of the poor. The prize distribution ceremony was held in University of Oslo, Norway on 10 December 1979, where Mother gave her acceptance speech.

Mother Teresa did not speak about her great works during her speech, rather she started it with a short prayer

and requested everyone to pray along with her. Mother then explained about the joy of giving. She said that giving love was the utmost service that one may do to each other and by doing good to mankind, we were showing our love for God who sacrificed everything for us.

According to her, God will judge us on the basis of our behavior towards the poor and the homeless. She further continued, "…he makes himself that hungry one, that naked one, that homeless one, not only hungry for bread, but hungry for love, not only naked for a piece of cloth, but naked of that human dignity, not only homeless for a room to live, but homeless for that being forgotten, been unloved, uncared, being nobody to nobody, having forgotten what is human love, what is human touch, what is to be loved by somebody…"

Mother stated that this love for the unloved people will make us holy and the privilege of this holiness is not limited to only a few people. Everyone who loves his fellow beings becomes holy in turn. She considers herself unworthy of this award and dedicates it to those hungry, naked, homeless, crippled, blind and diseased people who actually gave her the opportunity to love them and care for them.

She expected the award to bring an understanding between the rich and the poor. She considered it as a proof for the poor that God loves them and they are meant to be loved. They too deserve respect to lead their lives with dignity. It was in this speech that Mother Teresa advocated the dangerous effects of abortion and drew our attention to "the cry of the innocent unborn child."

She also explained the concept of love and the powerful impact it has on the lives of people. According to her, love has to be shared and spread to everyone. She said that Jesus resided in the hearts of every person whether rich or poor, therefore, if we love God we must love the poor. The power of love can eradicate the greatest poverty of loneliness from the face of the earth. In her own words, "Love begins at home. And love to be true has to hurt."

CHAPTER 20
Famous Quotes

Mother Teresa received the highest honor awarded to the civilians of India – the Bharat Ratna or the "Jewel of India" in 1980. Her words had a lasting impact on the listeners and had the power to put a balm on the agonizing souls of the distressed and lonely people who thought that they mattered to no one. Some of her precious sayings are as follows:

- The dying, the cripple, the mental, the unwanted, the unloved they are Jesus in disguise.
- If you judge people, you have no time to love them.
- Yesterday is gone. Tomorrow has not yet come. We have only today. Let us begin.
- Little things are indeed little, but to be faithful in little things is a great thing.
- It is not how much we do, but how much love we put in the doing. It is not how much we give, but how much love is put in the giving.
- I alone cannot change the world, but I can cast a stone to create many ripples.

- The most terrible poverty is loneliness, and the feeling of being unloved.
- Before you speak, it is necessary for you to listen, for God speaks in the silence of the heart.
- Speak tenderly to them. Let there be kindness in your face, in your eyes, in your smile, in the warmth of your greeting. Always have a cheerful smile. Don't only give your care, but give your heart as well.
- The hunger for love is much more difficult to remove than the hunger for bread.
- If you are humble nothing will touch you, neither praise nor disgrace because you know what you are.
- Do not allow yourselves to be disheartened by any failure as long as you have done your best.

- There is only one God and He is God to all; therefore it is important that everyone is seen as equal before God.
- I've always said we should help a Hindu become a better Hindu, a Muslim becomes a better Muslim, a Catholic become a better Catholic.
- If we really want to love we must learn how to forgive.
- Every time you smile at someone, it is an action of love, a gift to that person, a beautiful thing.
- Do not think that love in order to be genuine has to be extraordinary. What we need is to love without getting tired. Be faithful in small things because it is in them that your strength lies.
- What can you do to promote world peace? Go home and love your family.

CHAPTER 21
Doctrines of the Mother

Mother Teresa has been hailed as a living saint. She was a compassionate woman whose one aim was to spread love to everyone she came across. Her doctrines follow from her life and she preached what she practiced. The beauty of her soul is reflected in the innumerable deeds she did for the poor and the way she lead her life is the greatest example of the application of her teachings. Some of the beliefs of Mother Teresa have been discussed below:

- It is poverty to decide that an unborn child must die so that you may live as you like. If we pray, we will believe; if we believe, we will love, if we love, we will serve. We can do no great things; only small things with great love. You and I, we are the Church, no? We have to share with our people. Suffering today is because people are hoarding, not giving, not sharing.
- Jesus made it very clear. Whatever you do to the least of my brethren, you do it to me.
- Only in heaven will we see how much we owe to the poor for helping us to love God better because of them.

- Make us worthy, Lord, to serve those people throughout the world who live and die in poverty and hunger. Give them through our hands, this day, their daily bread and by our understanding love, give them peace and joy.
- I heard the call to give up all and follow Christ into the slums to serve Him among the poorest of the poor. It was an order.
- When a poor person dies of hunger, it has not happened because God did not take care of him or her. It has happened because neither you nor I wanted to give that person what he or she needed.
- In the developed countries there is a poverty of intimacy, a poverty of spirit, of loneliness, of lack of love. There is no greater sickness in the world today than that one.

- It's we who, with our exclusion and rejecting, push our brothers and sisters to find refuge in alcohol and become drunks. They drink to forget the deprivation of their lives.
- You will be surprised to know that in the poorest neighbourhoods in many of the cities where we live and work, when we get close to the people who live in shacks, the first thing they ask for is not bread or clothes, even though often they are dying of hunger and are naked. They ask us to teach them the Word of God. People are hungry for God. They long to hear his Word.

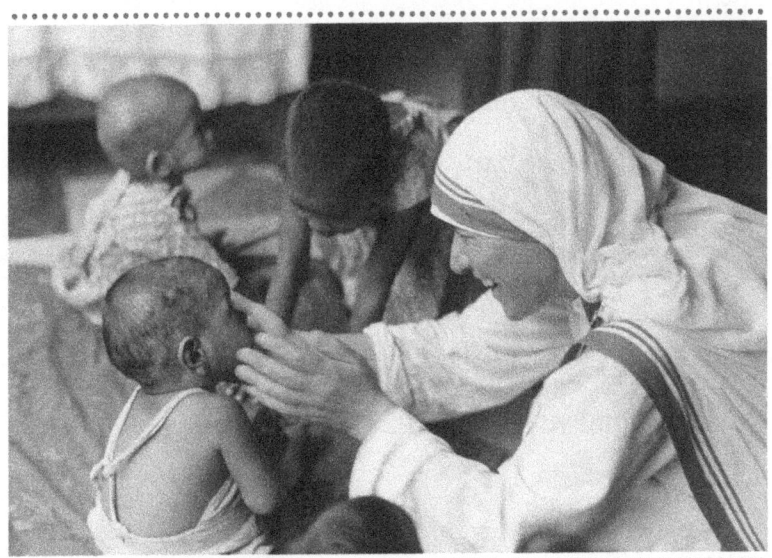

CHAPTER 22
Chronology

Aug 26, 1910

Anjezë Gonxhe Bojaxhiu was born in Skopje in Macedonia, the youngest of three children of an Albanian family.

1928

Leaves home for Dublin, Ireland, to become a Loretto nun. She takes the name Sister Teresa.

1929

Arrives in Calcutta, India and joins St Mary's High school to teach.

May 24, 1937

Takes final vows as a nun in Darjeeling.

1947

Most important event of her life, when she receives a call from Jesus to serve him among the poorest of poor and to live with them.

1948

Opens first slum school in Calcutta.

1950

Missionaries of Charity established.

1952

Opens Nirmal Hriday, or Pure heart, a home for dying.

1962

Receives the Padmashri award for distinguished service, her first award for her humanitarian work.

1971

Pope John Paul VI awards Mother Peace Prize.

1979

Gets the Nobel Peace Prize.

1980

Awarded India's highest civilian honour, Bharat Ratna.

1983

Has a heart attack while in Rome visiting Pope John Paul II.

1983

Queen Elizabeth II awards Order of Merit in New Delhi.

1985

Gets Medal of Freedom, the highest US Civilian award.

1989

Suffers a second heart attack. Doctors implant pacemaker.

1990

Wants to relinquish charge of Missionaries of Charity on account of poor health. But she is re-elected with only one dissenting vote, which was her own.

1991

Suffers pneumonia in Mexico, and undergoes heart surgery in the United States.

1993

Breaks three ribs in a fall in Rome.

1993

Another surgery in Calcutta to clear a blocked heart vessel.

1996

Fractures her left collar bone and is hospitalised.

Aug 22, 1996

Suffers heart failure, admitted to Calcutta's Woodlands Nursing Home.

Sep 16, 1996

Injures head in fall while getting out of bed; doctors detect spot on brain.

Nov 16, 1996

Granted honorary American citizenship.

Nov 22, 1996

Taken to Woodlands Nursing Home with irregular heartbeat.

Nov 29, 1996

Undergoes angioplasty surgery to remove two blockages in major coronary arteries.

March 13, 1997

Sister Nirmala elected to succeed Mother Teresa as leader of the Missionaries of Charity.

May 16, 1997

Arrives in Italy for a two-month tour and is given oxygen at Rome airport because of weariness.

June 18, 1997

Meets Princess Diana for fourth time at Missionaries of Charity residence in New York.

Sept 5, 1997

Mother dies following a heart attack at her religious order's headquarters in Calcutta.

Oct 19, 2003

Beatified at Saint Peter's Square, Vatican City by Pope John Paul II.

Sept 4, 2016

Canonized at Saint Peter's Square, Vatican City by Pope Francis.

www.ingramcontent.com/pod-product-compliance
Lightning Source LLC
LaVergne TN
LVHW091317080426
835510LV00007B/526